Especially for

....

From

....

Date

....

Written and compiled by Emily Biggers.

ISBN 978-1-61626-426-0

Scripture quotations marked NIV are taken from the HOLY BIBLE, NEW INTERNATIONAL VERSION®. NIV®. Copyright © 1973, 1978, 1984, 2011 by Biblica, Inc.™ Used by permission. All rights reserved worldwide.

Scripture quotations marked NLT are taken from the *Holy Bible*, New Living Translation, copyright © 1996, 2004, 2007 by Tyndale House foundation. Used by permission of Tyndale House foundation. Carol Stream, Illinois 60188, U.S.A. All rights reserved.

Published by Barbour Publishing, Inc., P.O. Box 719, Uhrichsville, Ohio 44683, www.barbourbooks.com

Our mission is to publish and distribute inspirational products offering exceptional value and biblical encouragement to the masses.

Member of the
Evangelical Christian
Publishers Association

Printed in China.

101 Ways to Make

Today
Great

BARBOUR
PUBLISHING

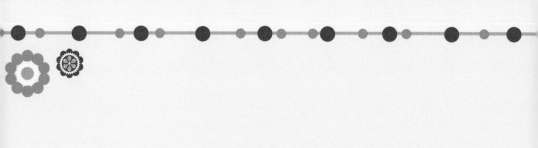

And God said, "Let there be light," and there was light. God saw that the light was good, and he separated the light from the darkness. God called the light "day."

GENESIS 1:3–5 NIV

Every day is a gift from God.
Make today great!

1.

Take a prayer walk and talk with God
as you enjoy nature and get some exercise.

To get up each morning with the resolve to be happy. . .
is to set our own conditions to the events of each day.
To do this is to condition circumstances instead
of being conditioned by them.

RALPH WALDO EMERSON

2.

Find a need and perform a random act of kindness. . .anonymously.

*Do all that you can to live
in peace with everyone.*

ROMANS 12:18 NLT

The habit of being uniformly considerate toward others will bring increased happiness to you.

GRENVILLE KLEIER

3.

Call an old friend that you've lost touch with. You'll be surprised how you can pick up right where you left off, no matter how much time has passed.

Beware the barrenness of a busy life.

SOCRATES

4.

Read a book to a child or

take flowers to a sick or elderly friend.

It only takes a few moments out of your day,

but it will be a blessing to another. . .and to you.

5.

Spend time outside

and thank God for His marvelous creation.

Attitude is a little thing that
makes a big difference.

WINSTON CHURCHILL

Believers, look up—take courage.
The angels are nearer than you think.

BILLY GRAHAM

6.

Stop for ice cream on your way home from work

or take the whole family

out for dessert after dinner!

Procrastination is the bad habit of putting off until the day after tomorrow what should have been done the day before yesterday.

NAPOLEON HILL

There is no passion to be found playing small—
in settling for a life that is less than
the one you are capable of living.

NELSON MANDELA

7.

Buy a book of stamps and some note cards.

Make it your goal to send a note to a friend or

relative every week. Start today.

Wisely, and slow; they stumble that run fast.

WILLIAM SHAKESPEARE

8.

Look at old photographs from

a happy time in your life.

Thank God for the past

and ask Him to bless your future.

You must do the thing you think you cannot do.

ELEANOR ROOSEVELT

9.

Turn the radio up loud.

Roll down your car windows. And sing!

At the end of your life,
you will never regret not having passed one more test,
not winning one more verdict,
or not closing one more deal.
You will regret time not spent with a husband,
a friend, a child, or a parent.

BARBARA BUSH

10.

Watch children laughing and playing on a playground. Better yet, go down the slide a couple of times yourself or see how high you can swing. You are never too old to play!

Fall seven times,
and stand up eight.

JAPANESE PROVERB

11.

Get a thirty-minute massage
for some much-needed stress relief!

Hold fast to dreams, for if dreams die,
life is a broken-winged bird that cannot fly.

LANGSTON HUGHES

We tend to forget that happiness doesn't come
as a result of getting something we don't have,
but rather of recognizing and appreciating
what we do have.

FREDERICK KEONIG

Commit to the LORD whatever you do,
and he will establish your plans.

PROVERBS 16:3 NIV

12.

Try out a new recipe if you feel like cooking.

If not, order takeout from your favorite place.

When one door of happiness closes, another opens;
but often we look so long at the closed door that
we do not see the one which has been opened for us.

HELEN KELLER

13.

Paint something–

a wall, your toenails, a picture–anything!

Everyone who got where he is has
to begin where he was.

ROBERT LOUIS STEVENSON

14.

*Eat fresh food today instead
of something that came from a package.*

Each day is a new canvas to paint upon.
Make sure your picture is full of life and happiness,
and at the end of the day you don't look at it
and wish you had painted something different.

UNKNOWN

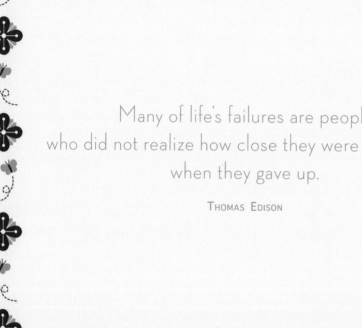

Many of life's failures are people
who did not realize how close they were to success
when they gave up.

THOMAS EDISON

15.

Try to speak only positive,

encouraging words today.

Remember to build others up rather

than tear them down.

It's kind of fun to do the impossible.

WALT DISNEY

16.

Pray for someone who
you have a hard time loving.

Time you enjoyed wasting
is not wasted time.

T. S. ELLIOT

17.

Take a long, hot, luxurious bubble bath.

18.

Let your neighbors know that you appreciate them by doing something tangible—mow their yard while they're at work, wheel their garbage can in from the curb, or take the newspaper up to their front porch.

Success is not the key to happiness.
Happiness is the key to success.
If you love what you are doing, you will be successful.

HERMAN CAIN

19.

Spend time today reading

your favorite book.

20.

Think like Andy Griffith and Barney Fife today. Even if you don't live in a small town, act as if you do—offer a friendly greeting to a stranger, hold a door for someone, or wave at other drivers on your way home from work.

Make it a Mayberry day!

*I have learned to be content whatever the circumstances.
I know what it is to be in need, and I know what it is
to have plenty. I have learned the secret of being content
in any and every situation, whether well fed or hungry,
whether living in plenty or in want.
I can do all this through him who gives me strength.*

PHILIPPIANS 4:11–15 NIV

21.

Do something special for someone you love.
Choose something you've never done before.
If you're not normally one to send flowers,
send them. If you've never written a letter
to someone expressing your appreciation
for him or her, do it today. Surprise someone!

The trouble with the rat race
is that even if you win you're still a rat.

LILY TOMLIN

22.

Write down ten things that you do well.

We're often too hard on ourselves,

so focus on your strengths today.

Be kind, for everyone you meet
is fighting a hard battle.

PLATO

23.

Perform a "smile experiment" today.

Smile at everyone you see.

How many smiles can you collect

from others in return?

Great minds have purposes;
little minds have wishes.
Little minds are subdued by misfortunes;
great minds rise above them.

WASHINGTON IRVING

24.

Exercise! Get your blood pumping.
It will give you more energy
and improve your mood.

25.

Clean one room of your home really well.
You'll be amazed how nice it is to enjoy
a clutter-free bedroom or kitchen!

26.

Be generous with grace today.

When someone cuts you off in traffic,

says something rude, or simply rubs you

the wrong way, show grace.

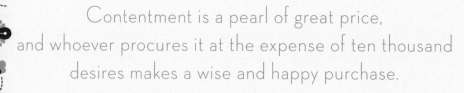

Contentment is a pearl of great price,
and whoever procures it at the expense of ten thousand
desires makes a wise and happy purchase.

JOHN BALGUY

27.

Indulge in a little splurge.

Eat some chocolate today. . .or something

that you try not to eat on a regular basis.

One tiny candy bar or a scoop of ice cream

has a lot of power to improve your day!

28.

Spend ten minutes today

expressing praise to God.

This is the day the LORD has made.
We will rejoice and be glad in it.

PSALM 118:24 NLT

The best and most beautiful things in the world
cannot be seen or even touched.
They must be felt with the heart.

HELEN KELLER

29.

Plant something in your yard or in a flowerpot—
a flowering plant or an herb, an aloe vera plant or
an evergreen tree. Whatever you choose to plant,
remember to care for it!

30.

Start reading a book and make it your goal

to finish it within two weeks.

Reading keeps your mind sharp,

increases your vocabulary,

and relieves daily stress.

31.

Think of a bad habit that is dragging you down.

Do you drink too much soda or smoke?

It takes only twenty-one days to form a habit.

Commit to twenty-one days without your bad habit

so you can have a better life.

Oh, the joys of those who do not follow the advice of the wicked, or stand around with sinners, or join in with mockers. But they delight in the law of the LORD, meditating on it day and night. They are like trees planted along the riverbank, bearing fruit each season. Their leaves never wither, and they prosper in all they do.

PSALM 1:1–3 NLT

Good humor is a tonic for mind and body.
It is the best antidote for anxiety and depression.
It is a business asset. It attracts and keeps friends.
It lightens human burdens. It is the direct route
to serenity and contentment.

GRENVILLE KLEISER

32.

Get enough sleep tonight

and see what a difference it makes.

Adequate sleep is essential for your body and mind

to perform at their highest potential.

33.

Be intentional about finding

a mentor and a mentee to enrich your life.

34.

Treat yourself to a small purchase today—

a tube of lipstick or a new CD.

Don't wait for your birthday.

Give yourself a present!

35.

Do something that hasn't been asked of you at work or at home. Go the extra mile. Do it out of kindness to others not for a reward or even a "thank you."

God is unchanging in His love. He loves you.
He has a plan for your life.
Don't let the newspaper headlines frighten you.
God is still sovereign; He's still on the throne.

BILLY GRAHAM

36.

Tell a joke or ask a coworker to tell you one.

Laughter is good medicine!

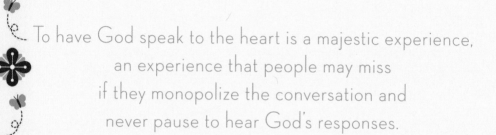

To have God speak to the heart is a majestic experience,
an experience that people may miss
if they monopolize the conversation and
never pause to hear God's responses.

DR. CHARLES STANLEY

37.

Take a different route to work.

A change of scenery will do you good.

Don't let yesterday use up too much of today.

CHEROKEE INDIAN PROVERB

38.

Eat a meal outside.

Have breakfast on your patio,

a picnic lunch in the courtyard,

or maybe grill some burgers for dinner.

39.

Stop by the nursing home and shake hands or give some hugs. Elderly citizens in your community will thrive on a simple hello and your kind touch.

40.

Wear a cool belt or a special piece of jewelry today. Sometimes the right accessory can pull an outfit together and make you feel more polished.

41.

Leave sticky notes around your home or office

to remind coworkers or family members that they

are special to you.

42.

*Memorize an encouraging scripture verse
or inspirational quote to help you with an area
in your life that you're struggling with right now.*

*Don't worry about anything;
instead, pray about everything.
Tell God what you need,
and thank him for all he has done.*

PHILIPPIANS 4:6 NLT

43.

Buy a container to help you become more organized at your home or office. Put it to work right away! Organization can save you a lot of time and can eliminate stress.

44.

Go to a garage sale—or plan to have one yourself.

Remember the old adage:

"One man's trash is another man's treasure!"

With the past, I have nothing to do;
nor with the future.
I live now.

RALPH WALDO EMERSON

45.

Read the comics in the newspaper.

Remember how you used to laugh at the

Peanuts gang and the Family Circus

as a kid? They're still there!

Take time to revisit old friends today.

We don't stop playing because we grow old;
we grow old because we stop playing.

GEORGE BERNARD SHAW

46.

Try a new cereal.

Break the monotony of your

"same ole, same ole" breakfast.

*Do not be overcome by evil,
but overcome evil with good.*

ROMANS 12:21 NIV

47.

Call for an "electronics fast" in your home

if you are a TV or Internet junkie—

or if you live with some.

Replace that time with

face-to-face family time instead.

48.

Take a drive through the country.

Roll down the windows

and breathe in some clean air.

Even better, go after dark.

You can see the stars!

Most folks are about as happy
as they make up their minds to be.

ABRAHAM LINCOLN

49.

Try a new hobby.

Is there something you've always wanted to do but have never taken the plunge? Sign up for a painting class or join a scrapbooking club. Whatever your dream hobby is, make it a reality. Try it!

Follow God's example, therefore, as dearly loved children and walk in the way of love, just as Christ loved us and gave himself up for us as a fragrant offering and sacrifice to God.

EPHESIANS 5:1–2 NIV

50.

Read a Proverb every day.

There are thirty-one chapters in the book of

Proverbs—one per day for a whole month!

I think I began learning long ago that those who
are happiest are those who do the most for others.

BOOKER T. WASHINGTON

51.

Get a manicure, pedicure, haircut, massage, facial, or some other special treat today. You deserve it!

52.

Plan a vacation.

Put it on the calendar and stick to it.

53.

Buy a new book of daily devotions or break out

an old one that has been on the shelf too long.

It will help you stay on track with your quiet times

and encourage your spirit each day.

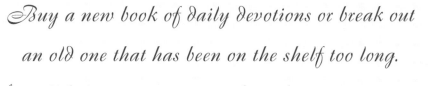

54.

Visit your local animal shelter.

Consider adopting a dog or cat that needs a home.

Pets are great company,

and they can become like part of the family.

It is pleasing to God whenever thou
rejoicest or laughest from the bottom of thy heart.

MARTIN LUTHER

55.

Volunteer as a mentor or story reader at a local public school. Kids need good adult role models. Just an hour a week could make a difference in children's lives!

56.

Go through the car wash today.

57.

Plan a reunion with old friends so that you can catch up. . .and repeat the same stories you've told for years. There's something to be said for those with whom we share a lot of history.

58.

*Make a to-do list of ten things
and do at least three of them today.
You'll feel a sense of accomplishment that will
inspire you to cross off three more items tomorrow!*

There are only two ways to live your life.
One is as though nothing is a miracle.
The other is as though everything is a miracle.

ALBERT EINSTEIN

But encourage one another daily,
as long as it is called "Today,"
so that none of you may be hardened
by sin's deceitfulness.

HEBREWS 3:13 NIV

59.

Check out a local theater.

Buy tickets for the next musical or play.

There's nothing like a live performance!

60.

Start a journal.

Recording your thoughts and prayers

can be therapeutic.

61.

*Make that doctor's appointment you've been
meaning to schedule. Your health is important.*

62.

Go out to dinner with a special friend.

Relax and enjoy some chat time.

The longer I live, the more I realize
the impact of attitude on life. . . .
We cannot change the inevitable. The only thing we can
do is play on the string we have, and that is our attitude.
I am convinced that life is 10 percent what happens to
me and 90 percent how I react to it.
And so it is with you. . .we are in charge of our attitudes.

CHARLES R. SWINDOLL

63.

When you get frustrated with inconveniences today, think about a friend or family member who would give anything to trade places with you. There's almost always someone whose circumstances make yours look better.

64.

Every now and then take a day off—
sleep late, eat your favorite foods,
do your favorite things,
and spend time with your favorite people.
Life is too short to miss out on your favorites!

65.

Pick up some doughnuts or another treat for everyone at your workplace. Surprise them!

The three things that are
most essential to achievement are common sense,
hard work, and stick-to-it-iveness.

THOMAS EDISON

66.

Send a thank-you note to a parent,
grandparent, teacher, or other person who played
a vital role in your upbringing.
Thank him or her for specific things
that influenced you.

67.

Ask for the crayons at a restaurant

even if there are no children in your party.

Everyone needs to color now and then.

It's good for the soul!

Love is patient, love is kind. It does not envy,
it does not boast, it is not proud.
It does not dishonor others, it is not self-seeking,
it is not easily angered, it keeps no record of wrongs.
Love does not delight in evil but rejoices with the truth.
It always protects, always trusts, always hopes
always perseveres. Love never fails.

1 Corinthians 13:4–8 NIV

68.

Pray while you drive today.

69.

Eat breakfast for dinner!

Whether it's biscuits, bacon and eggs, or pancakes,

this will be a yummy break in routine.

Of all the things Christ wants for us, loving Him and focusing our attention on Him are the most important.

DR. CHARLES STANLEY

70.

Get out in nature—take a walk, sit under a tree, go fishing, plant some flowers, or ride your bike on the trails at the park. Whatever you choose, breathe some fresh air today.

Above all, try something.

FRANKLIN D. ROOSEVELT

71.

Turn up the music and dance in the privacy of your own home today. No one has to know, and it will feel good to "get your groove on!"

Life is change.
Growth is optional.
Choose wisely.

KAREN KAISER CLARK

72.

*Go through your closet and fill
a bag of clothing that you haven't worn lately.
Drop it off at a local charity.
There are so many people who need clothing—
and a cleaner closet will be an added benefit!*

73.

Take a nap!

More than likely your body could benefit

from a little extra sleep.

When I stand before God at the end of my life,
I would hope that I would not have a single bit
of talent left and could say,
"I used everything you gave me."

ERMA BOMBECK

74.

Get up thirty minutes early.

Cook breakfast if you normally just grab a cereal bar

or use the time to read the newspaper or your Bible.

Some extra time in the morning may feel so good

that this becomes a habit.

A happy person is not a person
in a certain set of circumstances,
but rather a person with a certain set of attitudes.

HUGH DOWNS

75.

Think of three ways to save money

and put them into practice today.

You'll be surprised how these small money savers,

such as using coupons or cutting out expensive coffees,

will make a big difference to your bank account.

76.

Play a board game with friends or family members.
Video games may be more popular now, but nothing
compares to the interactions and laughter shared
during a game of Monopoly or Pictionary!

There are good days and there are bad days,
and this is one of them.

LAWRENCE WELK

77.

Clean out the in-box for your e-mail today.

It's so freeing!

Nearly every man who develops an idea
works at it up to the point where it looks impossible,
and then gets discouraged. That's not the place to
become discouraged.

THOMAS EDISON

78.

Walk through an upscale grocery store today

and try all the samples of yummy foods!

79.

Visit the public library.

Check out some good books or,

if you spend a lot of time in the car,

consider audiobooks on CD.

80.

Buy tickets to a professional sporting event or a concert. It will give you something fun to look forward to on those days when it's hard to face the pressures of work.

81.

Give yourself flowers today—or a bright balloon.

Both of these are easy to pick up at a local grocery

store and will provide a colorful touch

to your home all week!

82.

Learn something new—

register for an online college course or simply

log on to a website that will teach you

how to play chess. Be a lifelong learner!

Listen to the mustn'ts, child. Listen to the don'ts.
Listen to the shouldn'ts, the impossibles, the won'ts.
Listen to the never haves, then listen close to me. . . .
Anything can happen, child. Anything can be.

SHEL SILVERSTEIN

83.

Go to your local mall, pick a spot, and people watch. Better yet, go with a friend and make up fun stories about people in the bustling crowds.

Don't copy the behavior and customs of this world,
but let God transform you into a new person
by changing the way you think.
Then you will learn to know God's will for you,
which is good and pleasing and perfect.

Romans 12:2 NLT

You miss 100 percent of the shots you don't take.

WAYNE GRETZKY

84.

Search for Erma Bombeck quotes
today on the Internet. Read some,
and just try not to laugh!
This American humorist was
so gifted with humor.
Thank you, Erma, for making us chuckle!
Laughter is good for the soul.

I will be glad and rejoice in you;
I will sing the praises of your name, O Most High.

PSALM 9:2 NIV

Walking with a friend in the dark
is better than walking alone in the light.

HELEN KELLER

85.

Start a "thankful" journal.

Each day list three things you are thankful for

and soon you will have a grateful heart

in every situation.

86.

Do something that brings you joy—
play a round of golf, bake some brownies,
or pick up that guitar you have not played in months.
It's the little things in life
that make our days special.

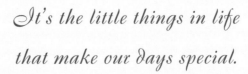

87.

Sing in the shower. . .or wherever you go today!
The Bible tells us to make a joyful noise
unto the Lord. It's okay if you don't have the voice
of a professional. God hears the heart of your song.

A bird does not sing because it has an answer;
it sings because it has a song.

CHINESE PROVERB

*Be kind and compassionate to one another,
forgiving each other, just as in Christ God forgave you.*

EPHESIANS 4:32 NIV

88.

Get yourself a new toothbrush today.

Make it your favorite color.

89.

Choose a funny picture to be the

new desktop on your computer.

90.

Make your bed even though you are just going to get back in it in a few hours. A neat bed makes your whole bedroom seem more "put together," and a tidy environment is so nice to come home to, isn't it?

91.

Look at your schedule for the day then cut it in half.
Now you are free to focus on today and do a few
things really well rather than stressing out
over an impossibly long list.

You are never too old to set another goal
or to dream a new dream.

C. S. Lewis

92.

Watch the sun come up this morning.

If you missed it already, watch it set this evening.

No one should miss either of these displays!

93.

Resist every urge to compare yourself to others today.

God knit you together in your mother's womb,

and He doesn't make mistakes!

People often say that motivation doesn't last.
Well, neither does bathing—
that's why we recommend it daily.

ZIG ZIGLAR

94.

Be fully present in every situation.
Resist the urge to chat on your cell phone while
you are in the grocery store checkout line.
Give your full attention to the store clerks.
You may be the only customer today who
asks them how their day is going.

95.

Organize one small part of your life today. Maybe it's a kitchen drawer or the bathroom medicine cabinet. Organizing in small doses makes a big job more manageable.

Live in harmony with one another.
Do not be proud, but be willing to associate
with people of low position. Do not be conceited.

ROMANS 12:16 NIV

96.

*Pay for the order placed by the person in the car
behind you at the fast-food drive-through window.
What a fun random act of kindness!
And who knows? Maybe it will
be passed on to someone else.*

If you can't make it better,
you can laugh at it.

ERMA BOMBECK

97.

Frame some favorite vacation photos or even some

pictures drawn by children in your family.

You will be decorating with memories.

98.

Focus on viewing change as

an opportunity for growth.

Change is inevitable.

How we respond to it is the part we get to choose.

Never, never, never, never give up.

WINSTON CHURCHILL

People who are unable to motivate themselves
must be content with mediocrity,
no matter how impressive their other talents.

ANDREW CARNEGIE

99.

Eliminate all excuses today.

100.

Set a new goal for yourself today

and track your progress till you achieve it!

I am only one, but still I am one.
I cannot do everything, but still I can do something;
and because I cannot do everything,
I will not refuse to do something that I can do.

HELEN KELLER

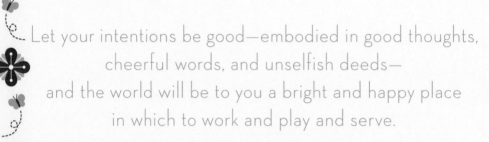

Let your intentions be good—embodied in good thoughts,
cheerful words, and unselfish deeds—
and the world will be to you a bright and happy place
in which to work and play and serve.

GRENVILLE KLEISER

101.

Make this your prayer:

Lord Jesus, make today a great day.

Help me to look for the good in others

and in Your world. Amen.